1 9 9

Daily Planner

With thoughts of joy
to brighten each day

Emilie Barnes

PAINTINGS BY

Glynda Turley

HARVEST HOUSE PUBLISHERS
Eugene, Oregon 97402

1997 Daily Planner

Eugene, Oregon 97402

ISBN 1-56507-427-0

Glynda Turley
P.O. Box 112
74 Cleburne Park Road
Heber Springs, Arkansas 72543

Art direction, design, and production by Garborg Design Works, Minneapolis, Minnesota.

Printed in the United States of America.

1997

JANUARY

S	M	T	W	T	F	S
			1	2	3	4
5	6	7	8	9	10	11
12	13	14	15	16	17	18
19	20	21	22	23	24	25
26	27	28	29	30	31	

FEBRUARY

S	M	T	W	T	F	S
						1
2	3	4	5	6	7	8
9	10	11	12	13	14	15
16	17	18	19	20	21	22
23	24	25	26	27	28	

MARCH

S	M	T	W	T	F	S
						1
2	3	4	5	6	7	8
9	10	11	12	13	14	15
16	17	18	19	20	21	22
23	24	25	26	27	28	29
30	31					

APRIL

S	M	T	W	T	F	S
		1	2	3	4	5
6	7	8	9	10	11	12
13	14	15	16	17	18	19
20	21	22	23	24	25	26
27	28	29	30			

MAY

S	M	T	W	T	F	S
				1	2	3
4	5	6	7	8	9	10
11	12	13	14	15	16	17
18	19	20	21	22	23	24
25	26	27	28	29	30	31

JUNE

S	M	T	W	T	F	S
1	2	3	4	5	6	7
8	9	10	11	12	13	14
15	16	17	18	19	20	21
22	23	24	25	26	27	28
29	30					

JULY

S	M	T	W	T	F	S
		1	2	3	4	5
6	7	8	9	10	11	12
13	14	15	16	17	18	19
20	21	22	23	24	25	26
27	28	29	30	31		

AUGUST

S	M	T	W	T	F	S
					1	2
3	4	5	6	7	8	9
10	11	12	13	14	15	16
17	18	19	20	21	22	23
24	25	26	27	28	29	30
31						

SEPTEMBER

S	M	T	W	T	F	S
	1	2	3	4	5	6
7	8	9	10	11	12	13
14	15	16	17	18	19	20
21	22	23	24	25	26	27
28	29	30				

OCTOBER

S	M	T	W	T	F	S
			1	2	3	4
5	6	7	8	9	10	11
12	13	14	15	16	17	18
19	20	21	22	23	24	25
26	27	28	29	30	31	

NOVEMBER

S	M	T	W	T	F	S
						1
2	3	4	5	6	7	8
9	10	11	12	13	14	15
16	17	18	19	20	21	22
23	24	25	26	27	28	29
30						

DECEMBER

S	M	T	W	T	F	S
	1	2	3	4	5	6
7	8	9	10	11	12	13
14	15	16	17	18	19	20
21	22	23	24	25	26	27
28	29	30	31			

January

SUN	MON	TUE	WED	THU	FRI	SAT
			1 New Year's Day	2	3	4
5	6	7	8 Vern- Dr. Kay	9	10	11
12	13	14 Dr. Kay Karen 9A.M.	15	16	17	18
19	20 Martin Luther King Jr. Day	21	22	23	24	25
26	27	28	29	30	31	

December/January

CLOSER

Every act
of kindness
moves to a
larger one
till friendships
bloom to show
what little deeds
have done.

JUNE MASTERS BACHER

DECEMBER

S	M	T	W	T	F	S
1	2	3	4	5	6	7
8	9	10	11	12	13	14
15	16	17	18	19	20	21
22	23	24	25	26	27	28
29	30	31				

JANUARY

S	M	T	W	T	F	S
			1	2	3	4
5	6	7	8	9	10	11
12	13	14	15	16	17	18
19	20	21	22	23	24	25
26	27	28	29	30	31	

DECEMBER

29 Sunday

✓Carol + Audrey to S.S. + Church w/us
↓
ALL P.M.

✓Sara + Renel 7:00 - 9:30

✓Carol overnite

1 Wednesday

NEW YEAR'S DAY

✓Marshall - New Years Auc.

✓Home eve.

2 Thursday

✓Laundry
✓Clean up

✓Tracy's Nursery faux painting

1997

DECEMBER

30 Monday

✓ Carol here til noon

✓ Stopped @ Rachaels P.M.

DECEMBER

31 Tuesday

To Marshall New Years Ave.

3 Friday

9:00 - Karen @ Tracy's Nursery - Hang paper border - Vern - Joyce

✓ Cleaned House Vern + I

4 Saturday

✓ Breakfast @ Essenhaus w/ Jay + Joyce

Jim & Jackie + family Pizza @ Chad + Tracy's

January

S	M	T	W	T	F	S
			1	2	3	4
5	6	7	8	9	10	11
12	13	14	15	16	17	18
19	20	21	22	23	24	25
26	27	28	29	30	31	

FEBRUARY

S	M	T	W	T	F	S
						1
2	3	4	5	6	7	8
9	10	11	12	13	14	15
16	17	18	19	20	21	22
23	24	25	26	27	28	

Seldom do we realize that the world is practically no thicker to us than the print of our footsteps on the path. Upon that surface we walk and act our comedy of life, and what is beneath is nothing to us. But it is out from that under-world, from the dead and the unknown, from the cold moist ground, that these green blades have sprung.

RICHARD JEFFERIES

5 Sunday

✓Sandwiches @ Burger King

✓6:00 Bertha Rhodes - Pic. - Church

✓7:30 Bob Evans w/Merrill + Shirley

8 Wednesday

✓Work on flyer
✓ " " Portfolio
~~Vern - Dr. Kay~~
~~Blood Tests~~
~~Spots on Arm~~

9 Thursday

7:00 a.m. - Karen Health check @ hosp.

✓Put 280 flyers out in boxes

1997

6 Monday

✓ Call 1806 - Hair Jackie
✓ Laundry
✓ Ironing
✓ Call - Shrock Homes?
✓ Portfolio?
Flyers?
✓ Call Joan Whitaker

✓ Supper to Katie & Memo
✓ Dessert - Rolls to Chad & Tracy

7 Tuesday

✓ 9:00 - Vern - Dr. Kay
✓ Call NBD - Greencroft
✓ Take records to Joan

✓ 7 P.M. Small Bus. Seminar - Essenhaus

Hosp. - Gary
(810) 762-8200
2105 Bd/1

Mary Brush - Nurse from Dr. Traynor's Office - (312) 908-2162

E. R. Miller Greencroft Teaching Computers @ Greencroft

10 Friday

✓ 10:am. To Joan @ Greencroft

11 Saturday

#1:00 - Amy Looker - Faux
3:00 - Carol Ebersole - Stencil

January

S	M	T	W	T	F	S
			1	2	3	4
5	6	7	8	9	10	11
12	13	14	15	16	17	18
19	20	21	22	23	24	25
26	27	28	29	30	31	

FEBRUARY

S	M	T	W	T	F	S
						1
2	3	4	5	6	7	8
9	10	11	12	13	14	15
16	17	18	19	20	21	22
23	24	25	26	27	28	

Fame is the scentless sunflower, with gaudy crown of gold; But friendship is the breathing rose, with sweets in every fold.

OLIVER WENDELL HOLMES

12 Sunday

✓ Merrills & Lowells here p.m.

15 Wednesday

✓ Clean up house

✓ Write Olivia lost tooth

✓ 3:00 See Amy Looker – faux Made estimate

✓ 6:00 Meet Rachael & Al "Plain & Fancy"

16 Thursday

1997

13 Monday

9:00 - To Carol Ebersoles to start "train" stenciling –

Rec'd. check from Belcher
✓ (500.–) K- (100.00)

14 Tuesday

~~9:00 - Dr. Kay
101 Mailyn Ave.
Suite 3
219-533-9009~~

9:00 Finished
53 ft. of Stenciling

Job ($286.20)
total incl. 10% discount

11 actual hours of Stenciling @ 6.00 ft.

53
6–
$318.–

$29.00
11 | 318–
22
98

26
11 | 290
22
70

17 Friday

8:30 Color-Cut

Leave for LaPeer –

18 Saturday

Herbs Auction
Vern & I
both help

January

The mute bird sitting on the stone,
The dank moss dripping from the wall,
The garden-walk with weeds o'ergrown,
I love them—how I love them all!

EMILIE BRONTË

JANUARY

S	M	T	W	T	F	S
			1	2	3	4
5	6	7	8	9	10	11
12	13	14	15	16	17	18
19	20	21	22	23	24	25
26	27	28	29	30	31	

FEBRUARY

S	M	T	W	T	F	S
						1
2	3	4	5	6	7	8
9	10	11	12	13	14	15
16	17	18	19	20	21	22
23	24	25	26	27	28	

19 Sunday

~~Home~~ from Herbs ~

✓ Visit Gary

22 Wednesday

✓ Sew 5 pillows
Cut out nearly
everything for
Carol Eversole
Vern - Painted
bulletin bd. +
make R.R. Sign

23 Thursday

✓ Behind
7 a.m. Hosp.
Community
Health Promotion

7-9 - Parish Resource Center
6:15 Banner workshop
Barb
Mary Ann
Connie Esch
Esther Thomas
Cindy Hawkins

1997

20 Monday

MARTIN LUTHER KING JR. DAY

✓ Dorothy & C. - Shopping

✓ Herb's Real Estate Auction -

✓ Home @ midnight

21 Tuesday

✓ Dr. Kay 9:30 Karen

✓ Laundry

✓ Order Carol Ebersole Stencil - 151 Sara's Ivy Andreaes Designs

✓ Lunch w/ Aunt Eddie & Janelle

✓ Shopping for Carol Ebersole 3hrs. (45.00)

24 Friday

✓ Clean Garage

✓ Dust House

✓ Walmart - Sale

~~Co~~

Sew -

25 Saturday

Finishing Sewing

Dee Birkey Stenciling 533-8392

✓ Write Gary
Write Herb & Dorothy

MMA
533-9515
Cindy Blue
ext. 281
Data Entry

~~Bench - Bombay~~
~~33" h~~
~~47" wide~~
~~18" deep~~
~~118.80~~
~~# 742515~~

January/February

JANUARY

S	M	T	W	T	F	S
			1	2	3	4
5	6	7	8	9	10	11
12	13	14	15	16	17	18
19	20	21	22	23	24	25
26	27	28	29	30	31	

FEBRUARY

S	M	T	W	T	F	S
						1
2	3	4	5	6	7	8
9	10	11	12	13	14	15
16	17	18	19	20	21	22
23	24	25	26	27	28	

Adam was a gardener, and God who made him sees That half a proper gardener's work is done upon his knees.

RUDYARD KIPLING

26 Sunday

29 Wednesday

11:00 a.m. Manamagram
Dentist appt.
1:00 Julie Zimmerman
Estimate – Julie 3.
Statement – Carol

Supper w/Rachael + Al @ Essenhaus

30 Thursday

10:30 – Carol ~~Shelly~~ Ebersole – Put Matthew's Room up...
~~Shelly's Faux Painting~~
~~10:00 @ Shelly's Base paint~~

1:00 Stencil Ready – Sue Graham
3:00 Dentist
7:00 Joe Miller
Julie ~~Zimmerman~~ Contract

1997

27 Monday

✓Sue G. Stencil
Carol E. - Dust Ruffle
classical music
10:00 Julie (great room)
Zimmerman
534-7353
2:00 Sue Graham
~~2:45~~ Dee
Birkey
533-8392
works w/ Janette Yoder
(stenciling)

28 Tuesday

✓Call Dr. Kay
Re: ~~#~~ polyp
on Cat Scan
533-9009
✓To Merch. Mart
✓To Chicago
Dr. Traynor
(Vern)

Select
Artificials
~~[illegible]~~ Wholesale
(314) 621-3050

Amy Looker
will get back
w/me on 28th
I'll honor
discounted
price

31 Friday

~~Shelly~~ ?
8:30 - Sue Graham's
Kitchen

Order Julie's
Stencils

Call Dr. Kay
Make Carol's
Stencil Compreh.

FEBRUARY

1 Saturday

✓Bridgette Coming
~~8:30 Prayer Group~~
~~@ Pat Yoder's~~

~~[illegible]~~
✓10:00 Bob Shriener

✓Ordered Julie's
stencils

Gary Cooper
Riverbend N.H
11941 Belsey Rd.
Grand Blanc,
(810) 694-1970
went in 1/24
2 wks. ?
RM

February

SUN	MON	TUE	WED	THU	FRI	SAT
						1
2	3	4	5	6	7	8
9	10	11	12 Lincoln's Birthday / Ash Wednesday	13	14 Valentine's Day	15
16	17 Presidents' Day	18	19	20	21	22 Washington's Birthday
23	24	25	26	27	28	

February

S	M	T	W	T	F	S
						1
2	3	4	5	6	7	8
9	10	11	12	13	14	15
16	17	18	19	20	21	22
23	24	25	26	27	28	

FEBRUARY

S	M	T	W	T	F	S
						1
2	3	4	5	6	7	8
9	10	11	12	13	14	15
16	17	18	19	20	21	22
23	24	25	26	27	28	29
30	31					

MARCH

I guess a good gardener always starts as a good weeder.

AMOS PETTINGILL

2 Sunday

Bridgelle here

Gift for Gwen's Baby Shower

5 Wednesday

Vern leaves for Chicago Hosp. @ 7:30

9:45 - Surgery PAC

Clean House

6 Thursday

Stencil Carol's Guest Rooms

5:30 Lent Planning Mtg. @ Church

1997

Clayton Miller
848-2251
call Monday

3 Monday

Bridgette here
Laundry
Ironing

4 Tuesday

w/ Bridgette
✓ To: Vicksburg
✓ Shelley's
Bathroom
✓ 4 1/4 hrs.
✓ $225.00

✓ Gwen's Baby Shower

Lenton
banner
for 4/16
mtg. this
week –

Paul
Esch will
call back
mon.

Ray Yoder

7 Friday

→

~~Stencil Carol's~~
~~Guest Rm.~~

w/ Rachael
South Bend
E. Michael Feltman
Endodontic
10:30 A.M.
✓ Root Canal

8 Saturday

→
~~To Rensse~~ ?
~~Come back~~
~~Sunday~~ –

~~Go to Chicago~~

✓ Infection
Swelled
Face

Gary @ Hedrick
Sharon's
1-810-640-
2184
6056 E. Frances
Mt. Morris 48458

February

Awake, O north wind; and come, O south wind! Blow upon my garden, let its fragrance be wafted abroad. Let my beloved come to his garden, And eat its choicest fruits.

SONG OF SOLOMON 4:16

FEBRUARY

S	M	T	W	T	F	S
						1
2	3	4	5	6	7	8
9	10	11	12	13	14	15
16	17	18	19	20	21	22
23	24	25	26	27	28	

MARCH

S	M	T	W	T	F	S
						1
2	3	4	5	6	7	8
9	10	11	12	13	14	15
16	17	18	19	20	21	22
23	24	25	26	27	28	29
30	31					

9 Sunday

To Chicago
Chad + Tracy + Me

Home @
9 PM

12 Wednesday

LINCOLN'S BIRTHDAY/ ASH WEDNESDAY

✓ 11:00 Meet @
Snyders 7353
Julie
Zimmerman
(2 hrs.)

✓ Make tableskirt
living Rm.

✓ Mtg. Banner
w/Barb

13 Thursday

✓ Make silk plant
Catalog

✓ Finish hemming Tableskirt

✓ Paint on banner

✓ meet Julie - 4 pm.

✓ To: Sam + Matties lights

1997

10 Monday

Vern discharged Sun. from hosp.
~~Home from Chicago~~
✓ Vern – bad day
✓ Stenciled @ Guest Rm. – Carol E.
✓ 7:00 Mtg. Lent

11 Tuesday

Stenciled all day @ Carol's Guest Rm.
~~4:00 Banner Mtg. @ church~~

Julie's Work – ?

Rachael Lee Art. Festival Mar. 21-22

Andi + Jon

718 832-7635

14 Friday

VALENTINE'S DAY

✓ 8:30 Haircut
✓ Clean House
✓ Fix Supper
✓ 10:30 – Vern haircut
John & Andi "Expo Roma" South Bend –

6:00 Dinner

15 Saturday

Help Vern Herb's on Auction

Jon + Andi

Make Banner for church 4:00 p.m. put up

Get rolls Sunday

February

FEBRUARY

S	M	T	W	T	F	S
						1
2	3	4	5	6	7	8
9	10	11	12	13	14	15
16	17	18	19	20	21	22
23	24	25	26	27	28	

MARCH

S	M	T	W	T	F	S
						1
2	3	4	5	6	7	8
9	10	11	12	13	14	15
16	17	18	19	20	21	22
23	24	25	26	27	28	29
30	31					

What is a weed?
A plant whose
virtues have
not yet been
discovered.

RALPH WALDO EMERSON

16 Sunday

Breakfast -
~~Craig~~ &
Jon & Andi
Family

12:30 - Doug &
Janettes

4:00 Chad &
Tracys

B.S. eve.

19 Wednesday

To Shipsee -
Antique
Shops

20 Thursday

Breakfast
w/ Shirley

Sewing -
Valance - Tracy

Carol Gerber
died 11:00 p.m.

1997

17 Monday

PRESIDENTS' DAY

Laundry

Order "Village" stencil

Order stencil Book

Shopping w/Tracy for Nursery

✓ 7:00 Lent Mtg @ church

18 Tuesday

11:40 Aunt Eddie picking me up for Brick House

6:30 Barb coming to see banner

Shirley M. B-day. 24th

Ellen Kaufman

219-825-9837

21 Friday

Change CA Plans - Order flowers

22 Saturday

WASHINGTON'S BIRTHDAY

SB to Chicago - depart #645 @ 12:45 (not 12:15) to San. Francisco Ar - 3:18

Lv. Mar. 1 San F. United 9:00 am #134 (new) to Chicago

Get ticket re-issued when we check in - Stickers

Called to give changes to us

February/March

FEBRUARY

S	M	T	W	T	F	S
						1
2	3	4	5	6	7	8
9	10	11	12	13	14	15
16	17	18	19	20	21	22
23	24	25	26	27	28	

MARCH

S	M	T	W	T	F	S
						1
2	3	4	5	6	7	8
9	10	11	12	13	14	15
16	17	18	19	20	21	22
23	24	25	26	27	28	29
30	31					

I know a little
garden close,
Set thick with
lily and red rose,
Where I would
wander if I might
From dewy morn
to dewy night.

WILLIAM MORRIS

23 Sunday

To Alonson

26 Wednesday

Vern - hosp.
Chicago

✓ Tracy's -
supper

✓ Vern home from
hosp.

27 Thursday

✓ Make board
for "Village"
for Carol —
✓ Get Quilt

✓ Proposal for
Sara

✓ Proposal for
Carol -
guest rm.
Meredith
Loons

1997

24 Monday

Carol's Funeral

home —

25 Tuesday

Call Julie Zimmerman re: farm board

Get wallpaper swatch grape colors

Look @ Quilt Snips

✓ Blood Clot Vern to hosp Goshen then to Chicago

Mary Showalter Mar. 24 hang paper

Call Clayton 848-2251

28 Friday

✓ Upholster Wicker Chair - LR Vern helped

✓ 7:00 To Donna & Marv's home

MARCH

1 Saturday

8:30 Prayer Mtg. @ Evans

~~Home from San Francisco~~

6:30 MYF Dinner Theatre 30^{00}

March

SUN	MON	TUE	WED	THU	FRI	SAT
						1
2	3	4	5	6	7	8
9	10	11	12	13	14	15
16	17 St. Patrick's Day	18	19	20	21	22
23 Palm Sunday 30 Easter	24 31	25	26	27	28 Good Friday	29

March

What sweetness is left in life if you take away friendship? Robbing life of friendship is like robbing the world of sun.

CICERO

MARCH

S	M	T	W	T	F	S
						1
2	3	4	5	6	7	8
9	10	11	12	13	14	15
16	17	18	19	20	21	22
23	24	25	26	27	28	29
30	31					

APRIL

S	M	T	W	T	F	S
		1	2	3	4	5
6	7	8	9	10	11	12
13	14	15	16	17	18	19
20	21	22	23	24	25	26
27	28	29	30			

2 Sunday

Bleeding ulcer

9:30 Vern to hosp —

Call Carol Ebersole -

Village-cost -
Work time -
Th.-Fri.?

5 Wednesday

Vern home from hosp.

~~Pick up Wig~~?

6 Thursday

✓ Vern + I Stenciling @ Carol E.

✓ To S.B. - Wig

1997

3 Monday

Hosp.

4 Tuesday

Hosp.

✓ I went to Nappanee
- coffee & end Table
✓ Glennda came

7 Friday

✓ Went to Flint Auctions

✓ 7hrs. @ Carol E. Stenciling finished

✓ Work on Tracey's baby Comforter

8 Saturday

Clean House → S.S. assign.

Matrox
Goshen Fabric

Vase?
Wreath?
accessory
Coffee Table?

Tracy B-Gift

March

What a pity flowers can utter no sound! A singing rose, a whispering violet, a murmuring honeysuckle—oh, what a rare and exquisite miracle would these be!

HENRY WARD BEECHER

MARCH

S	M	T	W	T	F	S
						1
2	3	4	5	6	7	8
9	10	11	12	13	14	15
16	17	18	19	20	21	22
23	24	25	26	27	28	29
30	31					

APRIL

S	M	T	W	T	F	S
		1	2	3	4	5
6	7	8	9	10	11	12
13	14	15	16	17	18	19
20	21	22	23	24	25	26
27	28	29	30			

9 Sunday

✓ Assign. S.S. Class

✓ Tracy & Chad came to Clinton Frame Church

✓ 6:00 Footwashing @ church

To Bob Evans w/Squealy's Merrills & us.

12 Wednesday

9:30 Clanton, Marcia Velma

10:30 Julie Z.

13 Thursday

Buy Julie's paint mud room (plum)

Kim – (312) 908-5400

1997

10 Monday

✓ Laundry
~~Start~~
~~Julia's fam~~
✓ Sew Tracy's B-Comforter
Call Katie Lambright
Call Annabelle
✓ " Rachael – Shirley M.

✓ Prep. for Consult
✓ 7:00 Consult.
w/Carol E. + Meredith – Room
Silk trees

11 Tuesday

✓ Call – Verda + Squeekie
642-4878
Call – Jeanette Y.

✓ Wash Windows all
✓ Van ~~Wash~~ clean Car

Re: Consult.
w/Carol ~
orig. border?
meredith?
Walk-thru
for silk trees
consult. for
room
arrangement
pillows
round Table

GARY

St. Joseph Hosp.
6056 E. Frances
Mt. Morris
48458
810 640 2184
810 762-8311
GARY
Rm. 4233

(Sharon Hendrick)
6056 E. Frances
Mt. Morris 48453
(810) 640-
2184

14 Friday

3:00 Girls coming
Pop – cheese, crackers

Dinner here

* Roast Pork Dinner

7:00 To Janettes
– ready for shower

15 Saturday

10:00 AM.
Tracy's Baby Shower

P.M. – S. Bend?

Pizza?

March

MARCH

S	M	T	W	T	F	S
						1
2	3	4	5	6	7	8
9	10	11	12	13	14	15
16	17	18	19	20	21	22
23	24	25	26	27	28	29
30	31					

APRIL

S	M	T	W	T	F	S
		1	2	3	4	5
6	7	8	9	10	11	12
13	14	15	16	17	18	19
20	21	22	23	24	25	26
27	28	29	30			

True friends visit us in prosperity only when invited, but in adversity they come without invitation.

THEOPHRATUS

16 Sunday

* Cinnamon Rolls
O.J. - Coffee

* Sun. Dinner
Lasagna
Salad (Toss)
bread (french)
ice cream?

Gary Cooper "Bird"

19 Wednesday

20 Thursday

1997

17 Monday

ST. PATRICK'S DAY

Left for Chicago ~ hosp.

Port-Cath in.

18 Tuesday

~~8:30 Color-hair~~

21 Friday

Home

22 Saturday

Vern very tired

Karen very tired

March

S	M	T	W	T	F	S
						1
2	3	4	5	6	7	8
9	10	11	12	13	14	15
16	17	18	19	20	21	22
23	24	25	26	27	28	29
30	31					

APRIL

S	M	T	W	T	F	S
		1	2	3	4	5
6	7	8	9	10	11	12
13	14	15	16	17	18	19
20	21	22	23	24	25	26
27	28	29	30			

To analyze the charms of flowers is like dissecting music; it is one of those things which it is far better to enjoy, than to attempt fully to understand.

HENRY THEODORE TUCKERMAN

23 Sunday

PALM SUNDAY

Very better
I went to
Church -

✓ To Jim + Jackie's
Took fabric

✓ Proposal - Carol
Meredith
✓ Sym. Cards -
Jill, John, Sharon
✓ Anniv. to Guenther

26 Wednesday

Julie's
Farm

8:15 - 12:15

to Supper
w/ Rachael +
Al -

27 Thursday

✓ Worked on
Carol's
Proposal

✓ Julie's
Stencil Comprehen
to her

✓ Select Carol's
Pink Color

1997

24 Monday

✓ Julie's Z.
job starts
"Great Room"
3hrs.

Call re: Jackie's fabric

Call re: plants

✓ Proposal for Carol re: Silks

25 Tuesday

Julie's Fam Job
A.M. 3½ hrs.
P.M 3

7:00
Membership class

✓ Call for haircut & color

Julie Z.
534-4448

Easter Dinner

Ham
Baked Pot.
Dev. Eggs
Rolls - Jackie
Ham Sauce - Jackie
Veg. - me
Salad - Kelly
Dessert - Tracy

28 Friday

GOOD FRIDAY

Clean House
"good"
V & K

29 Saturday

8:30 - meet Bart
9:30 - Sara

Groceries

Robert & Kelly here overnite

March/April

Deep in

their roots,

All flowers

keep the light.

THEODORE ROETHKE

MARCH

S	M	T	W	T	F	S
						1
2	3	4	5	6	7	8
9	10	11	12	13	14	15
16	17	18	19	20	21	22
23	24	25	26	27	28	29
30	31					

APRIL

S	M	T	W	T	F	S
		1	2	3	4	5
6	7	8	9	10	11	12
13	14	15	16	17	18	19
20	21	22	23	24	25	26
27	28	29	30			

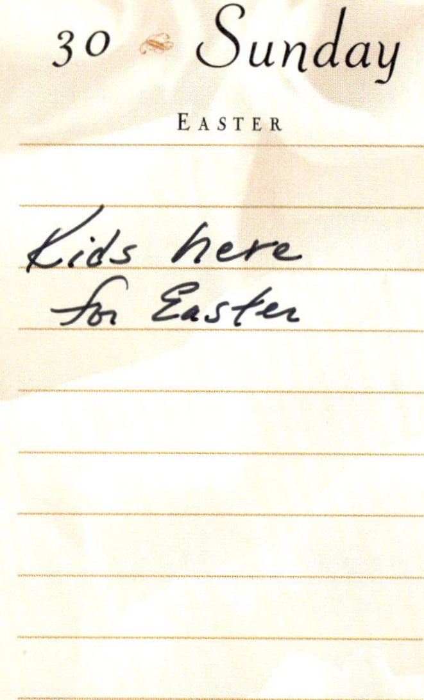

30 Sunday

EASTER

Kids here
for Easter

APRIL

2 Wednesday

Meredith's Stencil
could come
today

Stenciling - Julie's
Vern + I
all day

Final Order
on plants

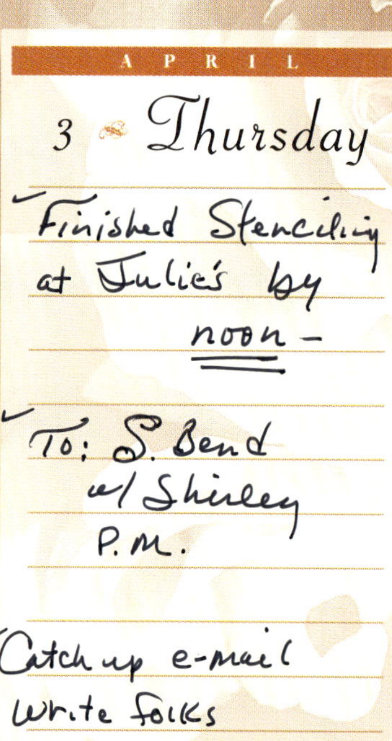

APRIL

3 Thursday

Finished Stenciling
at Julie's by
noon –

To: S. Bend
w/ Shirley
P.M.

Catch up e-mail
Write folks

31 Monday

✓ Start Stenciling Grapes - Julie Zimmerman

Vern to Hilman Ave

Order Plants?

APRIL

1 Tuesday

✓ A.M. - Stencil
Lunch w/Rachael

~~Vern - I~~
Stenciling

✓ Finished Bay Window Area -
7:00 Members Mtg.

APRIL

4 Friday

✓ Clean House
✓ Type Sale Bill (19th) & other ann.
✓ Schedule Hyatt Chicago?
✓ Hair Appt.
✓ Write Charlene Hopie

Get Foliage Book C cards

APRIL

5 Saturday

✓ 8:30 Prayer Group here -
Pat Y.
Laurie B.
Marsha?
Trisch Miller (Bob)
Fran
Ann M.
Devot. - Verda B
Mary Ann

✓ Sew Tracy's Crib Pads

Judy Patterson? nose bleeds!
Joy - Work?

April

SUN	MON	TUE	WED	THU	FRI	SAT
		1	2	3	4	5
6	7	8	9	10	11	12
13	14	15	16	17	18	19
20	21	22 Passover	23 Secretaries Day	24	25	26
27	28	29	30			

April

APRIL

S	M	T	W	T	F	S
		1	2	3	4	5
6	7	8	9	10	11	12
13	14	15	16	17	18	19
20	21	22	23	24	25	26
27	28	29	30			

MAY

S	M	T	W	T	F	S
				1	2	3
4	5	6	7	8	9	10
11	12	13	14	15	16	17
18	19	20	21	22	23	24
25	26	27	28	29	30	31

I am glad that in the springtime of life there were those who planted the flowers of love in my heart instead of thistles.

ROBERT LOUIS STEVENSON

6 Sunday

(Amish widow)
Esther Bender
S. eve. Serd.
Sister to Mary B. & Eli
Dean & Fanny Yoder's daughter married to Ester's brother

9 Wednesday

Paint Meredith's Room
5 hrs.
Janette - dinner (eve.)

10 Thursday

7½ hrs.
~~Stencil~~
~~Furniture~~

1997

✓ 6.A.M. - Vern to MI.

7 Monday

✓ Laundry
✓ Ironing
Get Sara's birthday card
21 - Jim
29. Tracy
✓ Pack - Vern
✓ Hem Pants
✓ Cement Ficus

8 Tuesday

Plants arrive?
✓ 10:30 Color + Cut - Ericka
Call Crown Mktg. Certif # 359544 to see if res. is confirmed → also check if more days are avail. @ Hyatt Regency
✓ Paint chip to Carol
✓ Comprehensive to CAROL
✓ 7:00 Members Class

813-535-6600

Tell Vern

6 qt. maple Syrup Chad

11 Friday

9 hrs
also for Carol
3/10 Consult.
$20.00

Pack for Fort Wayne

12 Saturday

Sondi gets married today

* Ray Yoder Farm Auction

April

APRIL

S	M	T	W	T	F	S
		1	2	3	4	5
6	7	8	9	10	11	12
13	14	15	16	17	18	19
20	21	22	23	24	25	26
27	28	29	30			

MAY

S	M	T	W	T	F	S
				1	2	3
4	5	6	7	8	9	10
11	12	13	14	15	16	17
18	19	20	21	22	23	24
25	26	27	28	29	30	31

In the garden,
after a rainfall,
you can faintly,
yes, hear the
breaking of new
blooms.

TRUMAN CAPOTE

13 Sunday

Sara's Birthday

16 Wednesday

To: Nappanee
for Plants, CAROL
12:00 Plain & Fancy
w/ Aunt Eddie
~~12:00 College~~
~~Japanese~~
~~Luncheon~~

17 Thursday

Work on Plants
Sewing Carol

Clayton's
Auction

1997

14 Monday

Order Jim's Shirt - Land's End

Card Out

✓ 9-5 - Stenciling Meredith's Furniture

Pick up 30" table fabric - Skirt 2 pillows

15 Tuesday

11:45 - College Church Japanese Luncheon

7:00 Member's Class

18 Friday

✓ 9:00 - Finish Stencil bed + bookcase

Put in plants

✓ Make Pink Bows

19 Saturday

✓ To Busk Brothers w/ Tracy

A.A. Consignment Auction

(Sue + Renel's Aunt Alma)

✓ Flower Arrangement for Carol E.

April

ARIL

S	M	T	W	T	F	S
		1	2	3	4	5
6	7	8	9	10	11	12
13	14	15	16	17	18	19
20	21	22	23	24	25	26
27	28	29	30			

MAY

S	M	T	W	T	F	S
				1	2	3
4	5	6	7	8	9	10
11	12	13	14	15	16	17
18	19	20	21	22	23	24
25	26	27	28	29	30	31

Oh see how
thick the goldcup
flowers
Are lying in field
and lane,
With dandelions to
tell the hours
That never are
told again.

A.E. HOUSMAN

20 Sunday

✓ M.Y.F. dinner @ church

✓ letters "Iola"

✓ ordered wrought Iron Fence Stencil

23 Wednesday

SECRETARIES DAY

✓ To: Vicksburg

~~Grant's~~ ~~Grandparent's~~ ~~Day~~ -

✓ (1) Shelly's faux

✓ (2) Jackie's Stencil (Bridgette's Furn.)

24 Thursday

✓ ~~Home~~ @ 10:00 a.m.

✓ 4 hrs. 1:00 - Julie Z. Coming here @ 1:00 to pick up ladder

Tracy's due date

1997

21 Monday

Tina's Birthday

22 Tuesday

PASSOVER

Chad & Tracy's Anniversary

7:00 Member's Class

Chad & Tracy's Anniversary

Vern's Cellular Phone

25 Friday

✓ Bake Muffins - freeze

~~Visit Annabelle~~

~~"Fern"~~

✓ note to Sally L.

✓ Take Tracy for birthday Outfit

26 Saturday

✓ Finish Window

✓ Groc.

✓ Work on Chair

✓ to Tracy's to see landscaping

April/May

APRIL

S	M	T	W	T	F	S
		1	2	3	4	5
6	7	8	9	10	11	12
13	14	15	16	17	18	19
20	21	22	23	24	25	26
27	28	29	30			

MAY

S	M	T	W	T	F	S
				1	2	3
4	5	6	7	8	9	10
11	12	13	14	15	16	17
18	19	20	21	22	23	24
25	26	27	28	29	30	31

The morning dawns with an unwonted crimson; the flowers more odorous seem; the garden birds sing louder, and the laughing sun ascends the gaudy earth with an unusual brightness: all nature smiles, and the whole world is pleased.

DAY KELLOGG LEE

27 Sunday

✓ Kent Miller in church

✓ Hacienda w/ Squeaky's Ray + Fran Ann + Ellis mast

30 Wednesday

To hosp.

Folks coming –

Supper (here) 6:00

8:00 – Birthday Party

MAY

1 Thursday

Aunt Eddie's Birthday

Folks leave –

Went to Tracy's

✓ Made dinner Spaghetti ~~Chicken + rice~~

Stayed overnite

Cellular Phone 517-370-2081

1997

28 Monday

Hang Carol's Mirror —
Take lamps over

Pick up ladder
@ Julie's

29 Tuesday

Alexa
Rae born
4:11 P.M.

-Vern's
Faith Story

7:00
Member's Class

Tracy's Birthday

Ord. lamp -
Meredith's
Room -

Carol's
Plants come
this week?

May 5 -
Verda's 50th

Marcia's - co-
worker - Jw.

MAY

2 Friday

To: Chicago
"Verz"

Janette
Stayed w/
Chad + Tracy
overnite -

MAY

3 Saturday

Prayer Group -
Ann Mast's

May

SUN	MON	TUE	WED	THU	FRI	SAT
				1	2	3
4	5	6	7	8	9	10
11 Mother's Day	12	13	14	15	16	17
18	19 Victoria Day (Can)	20	21	22	23	24
25	26 Memorial Day	27	28	29	30	31

May

MAY

S	M	T	W	T	F	S
				1	2	3
4	5	6	7	8	9	10
11	12	13	14	15	16	17
18	19	20	21	22	23	24
25	26	27	28	29	30	31

JUNE

S	M	T	W	T	F	S
1	2	3	4	5	6	7
8	9	10	11	12	13	14
15	16	17	18	19	20	21
22	23	24	25	26	27	28
29	30					

I smelt the violet in her hand and asked, half in words, half in signs, a question which meant, "Is love the sweetness of flowers?"

HELEN KELLER

4 Sunday

late p.m. - Went to Tracy's - 2 hrs.

Home from Chicago

7 Wednesday

✓ 8:30 Breakfast w/Shirley @ Bob Evans

✓ To: Tracy's - 6 hrs.

✓ Vern + I - ate @ Ponderosa

8 Thursday

Alexa - 9 days old!

1997

5 Monday

✓ Laundry
✓ Tracy's @ 11:00 a.m.
✓ Supper - Vern came @ Tracy's
Made Chicken & Rice
7 hrs.
✓ Type Sale Bill
✓ Faith Story

6 Tuesday

✓ 9:30 Haircut
- JACKIE 534-1806
✓ 9:00 - Jackie J. @ Tracy's

7:00 Homeowner's mtg. Assn. @ Greencroft Senior Center
✓ Fellowship Meal
✓ my Faith Story

9 Friday

✓ Clean House
✓ Bathe Alexa
✓ Baked Cookies & Bars
✓ Kelly, Lindsay & Olivia Came!
✓ Pizza @ Chad & Tracy's

10 Saturday

✓ Mother's Day Brunch
✓ Kelly & Girls left @ 1:30

To Tracy's 8:15 til 10:30 Babysit

May

MAY

S	M	T	W	T	F	S
				1	2	3
4	5	6	7	8	9	10
11	12	13	14	15	16	17
18	19	20	21	22	23	24
25	26	27	28	29	30	31

JUNE

S	M	T	W	T	F	S
1	2	3	4	5	6	7
8	9	10	11	12	13	14
15	16	17	18	19	20	21
22	23	24	25	26	27	28
29	30					

Spring unlocks the flowers to paint the laughing soil.

REGINALD HEBER

11 Sunday

MOTHER'S DAY

@ Jackie's
for dinner
Chads w/ Alexa
Glenndas w/ Kids
& Lon

14 Wednesday

Finish
Wicker
Chair

15 Thursday

Chicago

@ Hyatt
Regency

1997

12 Monday

✓Laundry

✓2:30 Diane Roth

✓3:30 Tracy's
– 5:00

✓7:00 Squeaky +
Verda

13 Tuesday

~~Chicago~~ ——

~~Vern - Stem Cell~~

~~Harvest~~

✓Bird Feeder
for Kelly

✓Lamp Shade –
Meredith

✓Wicker Chair
upholstery?

Ironing?

16 Friday

17 Saturday

Recd. for
Membership
tomorrow

Menno
to do
mail for
US + Harold's?

Blue –
Paint –
Sun Room?

May

MAY

S	M	T	W	T	F	S
				1	2	3
4	5	6	7	8	9	10
11	12	13	14	15	16	17
18	19	20	21	22	23	24
25	26	27	28	29	30	31

JUNE

S	M	T	W	T	F	S
1	2	3	4	5	6	7
8	9	10	11	12	13	14
15	16	17	18	19	20	21
22	23	24	25	26	27	28
29	30					

For lo, the winter
is past, the rain is
over and gone;
The flowers appear
on the earth,
the time of singing
has come
and the voice of the
turtledove is heard
in our land.
The fig tree puts
forth its figs, and
the vines are in
blossom; they give
forth fragrance.
Arise my love, my
fair one,
And come away.

SONG OF SOLOMON
2:11-13

18 Sunday

To be
Rec'd. as
Members

Brunch @
Goshen Inn
w/ Merrills
& Ala

Merrills
here in eve -
Tornado!

21 Wednesday

Took train
To Olivia's
Graduation!

Verns came to
Kelly's p.m.

Party for Olivia

Stenciled bunny
in Olivia's room

22 Thursday

home from
Chicago

1997

19 Monday

VICTORIA DAY (CANADA)

Laundry

✓ Tracy
here
overnite
w/ Alexa

20 Tuesday

4:00 a.m. –
To Chicago

hosp.
harvest
✓ Vern hospitalized
3 units
blood
✓ I stayed
@ Worcester
House

23 Friday

10:30 Grant's
Grandparents
Day
2:30 Colbys

✓ Vern left.
for Fairmont

24 Saturday

May

MAY

S	M	T	W	T	F	S
				1	2	3
4	5	6	7	8	9	10
11	12	13	14	15	16	17
18	19	20	21	22	23	24
25	26	27	28	29	30	31

JUNE

S	M	T	W	T	F	S
1	2	3	4	5	6	7
8	9	10	11	12	13	14
15	16	17	18	19	20	21
22	23	24	25	26	27	28
29	30					

I always felt that the great high privilege, relief and comfort of friendship was that one had to explain nothing.

KATHERINE MANSFIELD

25 Sunday

To church

Potluck

tired –

28 Wednesday

Sara's

29 Thursday

Sara's
½ day

1997

26 ~ Monday

MEMORIAL DAY

I left
for Fairview
Auctions
+ Stenciling
for Sara

27 ~ Tuesday

Sara's

30 ~ Friday

✓ Virg's left
✓ Cleaned ofc
@ A.A.

31 ~ Saturday

A.A.

To Atlanta
book
auction

Glynda Turley ©1995

June

SUN	MON	TUE	WED	THU	FRI	SAT
1	2	3	4	5	6	7
8	9	10	11	12	13	14 Flag Day
15 Father's Day	16	17	18	19	20	21
22	23	24	25	26	27	28
29	30					

June

The afternoon sun penetrated the mass of honeysuckle that covered the porch, and fell on my upturned face. My fingers lingered almost unconsciously on the familiar leaves and blossoms which had just come forth to greet the sweet southern spring.

HELEN KELLER

JUNE

S	M	T	W	T	F	S
1	2	3	4	5	6	7
8	9	10	11	12	13	14
15	16	17	18	19	20	21
22	23	24	25	26	27	28
29	30					

JULY

S	M	T	W	T	F	S
		1	2	3	4	5
6	7	8	9	10	11	12
13	14	15	16	17	18	19
20	21	22	23	24	25	26
27	28	29	30	31		

1 Sunday

home
from M. –

4 Wednesday

Kelly + d
went to hosp.

Lindsays
graduation!

5 Thursday

Didn't go
to hosp.

Aldine came
to visit Vern

1997

2 Monday

Sunday

3 Tuesday

~~9:00 Color & Cut - Jackie~~

To Chicago
Chemo
95 hrs.

train to
Kellys

Home

6 Friday

Kelly + C
to hosp.

Cake deco
for Logan
Birth.

7 Saturday

train to
hosp

home 8:45
p.m.
from Chicago

June

JUNE

S	M	T	W	T	F	S
1	2	3	4	5	6	7
8	9	10	11	12	13	14
15	16	17	18	19	20	21
22	23	24	25	26	27	28
29	30					

JULY

S	M	T	W	T	F	S
		1	2	3	4	5
6	7	8	9	10	11	12
13	14	15	16	17	18	19
20	21	22	23	24	25	26
27	28	29	30	31		

Of all the lovely treasures at the rainbow's shining end,

One brings lasting pleasure—

A dear and trusting friend.

ANONYMOUS

8 Sunday

Vern - very tired
M-Protein
.01
"Seldom gets this low!"
Praise God!
✓Tracy + Alexa here
✓Al + Rachael here

11 Wednesday

1:45 Dentist
Dr. Michael Beachy
533-5925
make cleaning appt.

12 Thursday

Sofa-Bed delivered?

6:30 - Marv. + Donna

9 Monday

Alexa
✓ Laundry
✓ Ironing
✓ Call Dee - left mess

✓ P.M. - To Nappanee
✓ Mirror
✓ Plate Holders
✓ Container for plants

10 Tuesday

✓ Call Diane Roth
Finish ironing

Plants - Outdoors
Make ivy wreath?
Pot Spathyphyllum
arrange Planter
fabric - runner?
Call Carol Ebersole

13 Friday

4:30 Haircut & Wax
534-1806

14 Saturday

FLAG DAY

Possibles?

Fancy Garden Room?

Make runner for Carol

Carol E.
Fax - 219-535-2690
Work - 535-2683
Home 533-0724

Merrillville - Home Designs Wall he

June

Life begins the day you start a garden.

CHINESE PROVERB

JANUARY

S	M	T	W	T	F	S
1	2	3	4	5	6	7
8	9	10	11	12	13	14
15	16	17	18	19	20	21
22	23	24	25	26	27	28
29	30					

FEBRUARY

S	M	T	W	T	F	S
		1	2	3	4	5
6	7	8	9	10	11	12
13	14	15	16	17	18	19
20	21	22	23	24	25	26
27	28	29	30	31		

15 Sunday

FATHER'S DAY

To Jackie -
Father's Day

Grant came
home w/us —

18 Wednesday

✓ Aleta

✓ Type
Sale Bill

✓ Vern - Blood Trans.

✓ Clean up house

✓ Finish runner

19 Thursday

8:30 Prayer Group
~~[illegible]~~ Essenhaus

10:00 To Carols
touch-up paint
runner

756-2424 2024 W. 81st Ave.

1997

16 Monday

✓ Alexa

✓ Laundry

✓ Grant

✓ Dick & Ruby Essenhaus

17 Tuesday

✓ Sew on runner

✓ Jackie came - (Birthday)

✓ Picnic on deck

✓ Jackie - I to "Everlastings"

✓ I went to Concord - ene.

20 Friday

To Fairview

21 Saturday

Auction Antique Shop - HL

Chad's Ofc. ext. 727

(219) 593-2156

Tracy - ISUB Teen Suicide class

Greenlawn 121

674-5905

Security Ext. 4258

Get CAROL EBERSOLE

June

JUNE

S	M	T	W	T	F	S
1	2	3	4	5	6	7
8	9	10	11	12	13	14
15	16	17	18	19	20	21
22	23	24	25	26	27	28
29	30					

JULY

S	M	T	W	T	F	S
		1	2	3	4	5
6	7	8	9	10	11	12
13	14	15	16	17	18	19
20	21	22	23	24	25	26
27	28	29	30	31		

When at last I took the time to look into the heart of a flower, it opened up a whole new world—a world where every country walk would be an adventure, where every garden would become an enchanted one.

PRINCESS GRACE OF MONACO

22 Sunday

Fairview

Carol K. - P.M.

Bob + Graces

25 Wednesday

Ord. Video 19.95 Visa "Total togetherness" marriage video 1-800-647-9400 Takes 4 WKS.

26 Thursday

Tracy's last day

Lunch w/ aunt Eddie

1997

23 Monday

Myra
8 a.m.
Rachael Lee
12:00

2:30 - Violet

24 Tuesday

~~Home~~
to Goshen -

Road Tags in

27 Friday

10:30 - See Triplex

11:30 Lunch
@ Pie Pantry

28 Saturday

~~Auction~~
~~Acres~~

Cumberland
Boys -
Sun. eve.
@ church
6/29

June/July

JUNE

S	M	T	W	T	F	S
1	2	3	4	5	6	7
8	9	10	11	12	13	14
15	16	17	18	19	20	21
22	23	24	25	26	27	28
29	30					

JULY

S	M	T	W	T	F	S
		1	2	3	4	5
6	7	8	9	10	11	12
13	14	15	16	17	18	19
20	21	22	23	24	25	26
27	28	29	30	31		

Don't walk before me, I may not follow,

Don't walk behind me, I may not lead,

Walk beside me, and just be my friend.

ALBERT CAMUS

29 Sunday

Vern left for Farmin

"Cumberland Boys"

JULY

2 Wednesday

Hem Wh. Slacks
Work on Vest

Vern home P.M. from Mi.

JULY

3 Thursday

To Chicago
Dentist
Ct. Scan of Sinuses

Fireworks @ Larimer Green
Blk. Squirrel Golf Course

1997

30 Monday

✓ Laundry
✓ Spring Brooke office
✓ Ironing
✓ Deliver Palms to Carol E.
✓ Tracey's
✓ Spade flower beds
✓ Water Plants

JULY

1 Tuesday

CANADA DAY

✓ 10:15 a.m. Cleaning (teeth) Dr. Beachy

Uncle Ernie died 10:30 PM – Fri. Viewing 1–9
11:00 a.m. Funeral Fair. Church

Helen Smith Greencroft 537-.4736
Pillow 25.00 labor

JULY

4 Friday

INDEPENDENCE DAY

JULY

5 Saturday

~~Rack Fan~~
~~Chicago~~

5:15–6:00 Oakwood Inn

Glynda Turley
©1991

July

SUN	MON	TUE	WED	THU	FRI	SAT
		1 Canada Day	2	3	4 Independence Day	5
6	7	8	9	10	11	12
13	14	15	16	17	18	19
20	21	22	23	24	25	26
27	28	29	30	31		

July

JULY

S	M	T	W	T	F	S
		1	2	3	4	5
6	7	8	9	10	11	12
13	14	15	16	17	18	19
20	21	22	23	24	25	26
27	28	29	30	31		

AUGUST

S	M	T	W	T	F	S
					1	2
3	4	5	6	7	8	9
10	11	12	13	14	15	16
17	18	19	20	21	22	23
24	25	26	27	28	29	30
31						

I feel certain that almost every American must have a favorite childhood memory of picking flowers—dandelions on a lawn, perhaps, or daisies and buttercups in a meadow, trailing arbutus on a cold New England hillside in spring, a bunch of sweet peas in a hot July garden after admonishments from an adult to cut the stems long.

KATHERINE S. WHITE

6 Sunday

"Laying on of hands Serv."

Fran + Ray here + Rachel + Al -

9 Wednesday

✓ 8:15 - Breakfast w/Shelley

10 Thursday

8:45 Chicago

Transplant

1997

7 Monday

✓ Sale Bill –

✓ To Nappanee
window w/ boxes

✓ To Chicago
Dentist - Vern
Root Canal
3 fillings

8 Tuesday

✓ Leaphus fabric
Cut out blouse

5:00 Essenhaus
w/ Herb's
Phils

Mtg. @ Al's –
SS.

11 Friday

12 Saturday

VERN'S ROOM 312-908-3735

July

NW Mem. Hosp.
Wesley Pavilion
Rm. # 1462
Chicago, IL
60611

When the sun declined toward the west afternoon, I sat in the shade and from the veranda turned the hose with its fine sprinkler all over the garden. Oh, the joy of it! The delicious scents from earth and leaves, the glitter of drops on the young green, the gratitude of all the plants at the refreshing bath and draught of water!

CELIA THAXTER

JULY

S	M	T	W	T	F	S
		1	2	3	4	5
6	7	8	9	10	11	12
13	14	15	16	17	18	19
20	21	22	23	24	25	26
27	28	29	30	31		

AUGUST

S	M	T	W	T	F	S
					1	2
3	4	5	6	7	8	9
10	11	12	13	14	15	16
17	18	19	20	21	22	23
24	25	26	27	28	29	30
31						

13 Sunday

✓ Bad Cold!
✓ Olivia here to Tracy's overnite
Come home w/ AL & RACHAEL from Chicago

16 Wednesday

8:00 - Jackie + Glenda going to Chicago
✓ I stayed here ~~I'll go w/ them~~
✓ Bills pd.
✓ Cleaned house
✓ 3:00 Perm
✓ 5:00 Alexa
✓ Iron

17 Thursday

✓ 6:30 Walk 2+ mi.
✓ 1 load laundry
Finish ironing
Prepare w/portfolio
1 PM - Glennda Sentell
533-8305
Stenciling
Sew Vest?
Do nails
Call Dee Dickey
Call Carol Eversole

Buy white & pink wax begonias.

PERM

1997

FAX 312 908 2343

14 Monday

Olivia to Jackie's

Call Rachael - See 7/21 →

Home -

15 Tuesday

9:30 - Dr. Kay possibly reduce Inderal

work w/Rachael Home

18 Friday

Pack

Water plant Leave for Chicago

19 Saturday

Mary Bruech (312) 908 6999
Pager # 57802
hang on line

Fri
~~School Homes-Dike 534-2196~~

~~Debra Hayes Main 290 800-442-2345 143~~

July

JULY

S	M	T	W	T	F	S
		1	2	3	4	5
6	7	8	9	10	11	12
13	14	15	16	17	18	19
20	21	22	23	24	25	26
27	28	29	30	31		

AUGUST

S	M	T	W	T	F	S
					1	2
3	4	5	6	7	8	9
10	11	12	13	14	15	16
17	18	19	20	21	22	23
24	25	26	27	28	29	30
31						

Then, wriggling our toes in the mud like eight-year-olds, we closed the garden gate, wiped our feet on the lawn grass, lifted our faces, eyes shut, mouths wide, drank the rain as it fell, and were one with grass and trees.

HAL BORLAND

20 Sunday

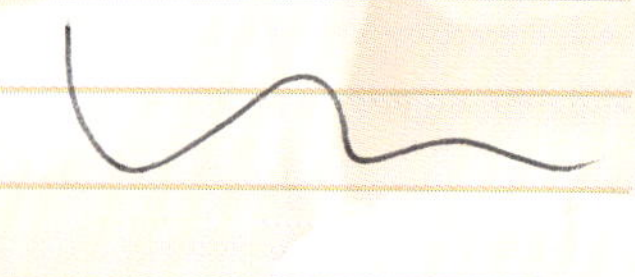

Come home w/Chad + Tracy

23 Wednesday

24 Thursday

1997

21 Monday

Call Rachael -
make Invitations
for boat ride
7/27 S.S.
North Webster
Boat Ride
Popcorn
Drinks
Cost?

Misplaced

22 Tuesday

25 Friday

26 Saturday

Reunion @
Eric Stoltzfus
Paula called
All their fam.
" Lee's "

July/August

JULY

S	M	T	W	T	F	S
		1	2	3	4	5
6	7	8	9	10	11	12
13	14	15	16	17	18	19
20	21	22	23	24	25	26
27	28	29	30	31		

AUGUST

S	M	T	W	T	F	S
					1	2
3	4	5	6	7	8	9
10	11	12	13	14	15	16
17	18	19	20	21	22	23
24	25	26	27	28	29	30
31						

In the dooryard
fronting an old
farm-house near the
white-wash'd
palings,
Stands the lilac-
bush tall-growing
with heart-shaped
leaves of rich green,
With many a
pointed blossom
rising delicate, with
the perfume strong
I love,
With every leaf
a miracle.

WALT WHITMAN

27 Sunday

Check w/Rachael
re: postage

Call Amy Looker
re: plants
foyer
(She has flyer)

Vern
released
hosp

Overnite
@ Kelly's

30 Wednesday

Alexa - 3-6

~~2-3:00~~
~~Glenda Sentell~~
~~533-8305~~

31 Thursday

Laundry

Type Sale Bill

4 PM - Diane
Roth -
bringing fabric
over -

1997

28 Monday

Home [illegible]
2:30

29 Tuesday

534-1806
11:00 First Impressions
Haircut & Wax
Color

~~4:00-4:30~~
~~Glennda Sentell~~
~~533-8305~~

AUGUST

1 Friday

AUGUST

2 Saturday

~~Helen Smith~~

Diane Roth
533-1331

Call Dee Birkey
533-8392

Amy Looker
next. mon.

Glennda Sentell
533-8305

Carla Whitaker
Sea Creatures

Glynda Turley

August

SUN	MON	TUE	WED	THU	FRI	SAT
					1	2
3	4	5	6	7	8	9
10	11	12	13	14	15	16
17	18	19	20	21	22	23
24 / 31	25	26	27	28	29	30

August

AUGUST

S	M	T	W	T	F	S
					1	2
3	4	5	6	7	8	9
10	11	12	13	14	15	16
17	18	19	20	21	22	23
24	25	26	27	28	29	30
31						

SEPTEMBER

S	M	T	W	T	F	S
	1	2	3	4	5	6
7	8	9	10	11	12	13
14	15	16	17	18	19	20
21	22	23	24	25	26	27
28	29	30				

What a desolate place would be a world without flowers! It would be a face without a smile; a feast without a welcome.

CLARA L. BALFOUR

Carol E. –
I Suggested
new brass 2 ?
cat. for ferns?
foyer

Pick up palms
Aug-10-17

3 Sunday

6 Wednesday

Sewed
Window
Treatments

7 Thursday

~~[illegible]~~
Auction
Posen

1997

4 Monday

Call Amy
Looker
533-1836
2 plants
or trees
Containers?

To -
Fairmont

5 Tuesday

~~10:30 Dentist~~
~~Dr. Michael~~
~~Beachy~~
~~fillings~~

Helped
Mom pack

8 Friday

Sew

Lunch
w/ Sara

Supper
w/ Rachel +
Sara

9 Saturday

Home to
Goshen

August

Friendship is precious, not only in the shade, but in the sunshine of life.

THOMAS JEFFERSON

Worship
Visual Comm.

Esther T. - C
Karen G
Gwen D.
Arlene M.

AUGUST

S	M	T	W	T	F	S
					1	2
3	4	5	6	7	8	9
10	11	12	13	14	15	16
17	18	19	20	21	22	23
24	25	26	27	28	29	30
31						

SEPTEMBER

S	M	T	W	T	F	S
	1	2	3	4	5	6
7	8	9	10	11	12	13
14	15	16	17	18	19	20
21	22	23	24	25	26	27
28	29	30				

10 Sunday

Call Amy Looker

✓ Call Annabelle Re: Becky

13 Wednesday

Rachael's gift

✓ 1:30 Haircut

✓ Call Amy

✓ Leta - Estimate

~~Call Carol E.~~

Make Comprehensives for Dee B.

✓ Vernoques to MI

14 Thursday

10-3- Alexa

~~NBC - announcing Publ. Clearing House Winner Tom Brokaw Call 1-800-443-0660 if not here Call by Aug. 12~~

1997

11 Monday

Laundry
Make Vern's Appt.
~~To Diane Roth's Hang Window Treatments~~
Ironing
3:00 p.m. - Dee Birkey
4:45 Folks
bringing land
- veg. - supper

12 Tuesday

Vern - Bld. Tests Goshen Hosp.
Help Dad
hang blinds
Lowe's
Meet Tracy @ photography
~~3:30 Color~~

15 Friday

11:30 Valentine
12:30 - Blood
- 6:00 Mail

16 Saturday

Rachael took me out to lunch
Cottage Garden
"Tea for 2"
Fun

Pending Clients

Diane Roth - Sewing
Amy Looker - Plants
Carol Ebersole - plan
Dee Birkey - faux
Lota - plants
Becky B. Stencil

Mary Ann Fishman

312-908-7243
56510

FAX
312 908-2343

Primary Care Practice
848-5484

Mercy Hosp. Grayling

August

True friendship is the priceless gift of seeing with the heart rather than with the eyes.

HUGH BLACK

AUGUST

S	M	T	W	T	F	S
					1	2
3	4	5	6	7	8	9
10	11	12	13	14	15	16
17	18	19	20	21	22	23
24	25	26	27	28	29	30
31						

SEPTEMBER

S	M	T	W	T	F	S
	1	2	3	4	5	6
7	8	9	10	11	12	13
14	15	16	17	18	19	20
21	22	23	24	25	26	27
28	29	30				

17 Sunday

Lunch in evening

3 P.M. - Jackie & Bridgette Coming overnite

20 Wednesday

Dr. Traynor 10:40 A.M.

To Kelly's? Choose carpet for office? Plants

21 Thursday

Rese four Bathroom

18 Monday
57 years!
Jackie +
Bridgette
here
Lunch -
Call aldik
Call Amy?

Vern ~ home
from MZ.

19 Tuesday
Vern's Birthday
60 years

Dee's Fam
Bedroom?

Mary
Brush
(312) 908-
2162

22 Friday
To Fairview
w/Al's 12:15
Help folks

23 Saturday

home -
Sat. Inc

Diane
Roth

August

AUGUST

S	M	T	W	T	F	S
					1	2
3	4	5	6	7	8	9
10	11	12	13	14	15	16
17	18	19	20	21	22	23
24	25	26	27	28	29	30
31						

SEPTEMBER

S	M	T	W	T	F	S
	1	2	3	4	5	6
7	8	9	10	11	12	13
14	15	16	17	18	19	20
21	22	23	24	25	26	27
28	29	30				

We make a living by what we get, but we make a life by what we give.

WINSTON CHURCHILL

24 Sunday

7:30 A.M.
Usher Mtg.
Sark—

27 Wednesday

✓ Type Sale bill
✓ letter to Carol E.
✓ Proposal to Amy Looker
✓ Hang Drapes
1:00 Diane Roth
✓ Help Mom w/ upper cupboards

28 Thursday

11:00–5:00 Took Mom & Dad to get TV & Kitchen Table & Chairs
✓ Helped Dad hang pictures
✓ Ordered Grass

1997

25 Monday

8:30
✓ Finish Faux
@ Dee Birkey's

26 Tuesday

~~Hang Drapes~~?

✓ To: Accents
Disc.
✓ To: Light Gallery
Disc.
6:00 Folks
moving In

Jim Coming

✓ School
Kits
16 80

Aldik - Sending
4 diffenbachia
Sitting Boy

Pending
Clients

~~Dee Birkey~~
~~faux~~

~~Diane Roth~~
~~sewing~~

Amy Looker
- plants - access.

Leta Gerber -
Plants
Oct.

Becky Bontrager
- Stencil

Carol Ebersole
- plants

Diane Roth
Plants

29 Friday

✓ Clean House
✓ Clean Mirrors
✓ Finish Laundry
Re-plant flowers?
Ironing
Buy Paint + Crackle for
windows
✓ Get Wedding
Card - money
✓ Groc
✓ Tracy here for Supper
✓ Folk IV. this
A.M.

30 Saturday

✓ Vern make flip-outs
in bathroom?

✓ 2:00 Wedding
Duane + Arma's
daughter
@ Nappanee

✓ Work on
Mom's Cupboards

August/September

AUGUST

S	M	T	W	T	F	S
					1	2
3	4	5	6	7	8	9
10	11	12	13	14	15	16
17	18	19	20	21	22	23
24	25	26	27	28	29	30
31						

SEPTEMBER

S	M	T	W	T	F	S
	1	2	3	4	5	6
7	8	9	10	11	12	13
14	15	16	17	18	19	20
21	22	23	24	25	26	27
28	29	30				

If you love someone you will be loyal to him no matter what the cost. You will always believe in him, always expect the best of him, and always stand your ground in defending him.

I CORINTHIANS 13:7 TLB

31 Sunday

✓ Pay
School Kits
$16.80

SEPTEMBER

3 Wednesday

✓ Elder Beerman
will call &
bring T.V. 1:30–3:30

✓ Ironing
✓ Deliver Carol E.
Put Photo album
& pic. in pickup
to work on up
north

✓ call Esther T.
✓ " Dwight Sark
✓ " Carol Maxwell
✓ " Jackie

SEPTEMBER

4 Thursday

Vern & J leaves
for Fairview

2 ferns w/
2 Salisbury lend

1997

SEPTEMBER

1 Monday
LABOR DAY

✓ Laundry

Finish Mom's Cupboard arrange.

✓ To Concord p.m.

✓ Put plants 5 in foam

✓ Putter Golf

SEPTEMBER

2 Tuesday

✓ Put Amy L. plants together

✓ Paint Windows (for Sale)

✓ Dick H. birthday 9/10

✓ Call first
6:00 Barbara K. Dinner

✓ Marv. & Donna's Dessert - Cards

To Do:

Deliver Amy's Statue?
2 Spathyphyllum w/ urns
1 Dieffenbachia

Diane's Roth
Fern w/ brass?
Dieffenbachia w/ brass

Start Lela's Order —
Deliver last Sept. 1st Oct.

Make up Stencil for Becky Bontrager

~~Carol E.?~~
~~2 ferns containers?~~

~~Work on Euro. Windows~~

SEPTEMBER

5 Friday

~~12:00 lv. for~~ Fairview

SEPTEMBER

6 Saturday

Folk's Auction

September

SUN	MON	TUE	WED	THU	FRI	SAT
	1 Labor Day	2	3	4	5	6
7	8	9	10	11	12	13
14	15	16	17	18	19	20
21	22	23	24	25	26	27
28	29	30				

September

For man, autumn
is a time of harvest,
a gathering together.

For nature, it is a
time of sowing,
of scattering abroad.

EDWIN WAY TEALE

SEPTEMBER

S	M	T	W	T	F	S
	1	2	3	4	5	6
7	8	9	10	11	12	13
14	15	16	17	18	19	20
21	22	23	24	25	26	27
28	29	30				

OCTOBER

S	M	T	W	T	F	S
			1	2	3	4
5	6	7	8	9	10	11
12	13	14	15	16	17	18
19	20	21	22	23	24	25
26	27	28	29	30	31	

7 Sunday

~~Usher~~

Coming home
from FairView

~~Usher~~
~~E-Sheild~~

10 Wednesday

✓ To Mall
w/ Shirley 8:15

~~534-1806~~

~~1:30 Amy's~~
~~Lookers~~

11 Thursday

✓ Set 2 Dieffen.
✓ Groom "
✓ Make price
list
✓ Lunch w/ folks
✓ Call Carol E.
✓ Call Cottage
Crafters

Windows 30—
plain

stenc. 40—

Shutters 60—

1997

8 Monday

✓ Laundry

✓ Ivy Arrange. on Sculpture - Amy L.

✓ Ivy on my Sculpture

✓ To Walmart

✓ Clean House

✓ Junk Out

Call Donald King 642-3165

✓ Tracy's - Supper

✓ Hang Alexa's pic.

9 Tuesday

✓ Prepare Bill - Amy Looker

~~10:45 Dr. Kay for ears~~

✓ Pick up Bulletins @ Church

✓ Kim's birthday

✓ Bro. Sis. letter

✓ 6:00 Church Visual Arts committee

New!

Aldik

214-749 0257

Ceramic

10" 12"

8 or 9" high

moss

Burgundy

taupe

1" w/gold

12 Friday

✓ Call Amy Looker re: time

✓ Deliver

1 statue

2 - Spath w/ urns

1 - Dieff in sm. Tuscany

✓ Paint Vases. Becky B.

✓ Auction - Harald's parents place

✓ Finish Laundry

13 Saturday

September

SEPTEMBER

S	M	T	W	T	F	S
	1	2	3	4	5	6
7	8	9	10	11	12	13
14	15	16	17	18	19	20
21	22	23	24	25	26	27
28	29	30				

OCTOBER

S	M	T	W	T	F	S
			1	2	3	4
5	6	7	8	9	10	11
12	13	14	15	16	17	18
19	20	21	22	23	24	25
26	27	28	29	30	31	

A little
word in kindness
spoken,
a motion or a tear;
has often
healed the heart
that's broken,
and made a
friend sincere.

DANIEL CLEMENT
COLESWORTHY

14 Sunday

Usher –

17 Wednesday

Dad's Birthday

11:00 Haircut
& Wax
534-1806

* Key – @ Carol Ebersole's
2:00 p.m.

7:00 Mtg.
Harvest Sun.
@ Church.

Pat Yoder & I –
Promotion

18 Thursday

9:00 Dentist

2:30 Dr. Schmucker
(Vern)

1997

15 Monday

7:00
Carol Ebersole

16 Tuesday

19 Friday

8:45 Jackie -
Carol Ebersoles

20 Saturday

Meeting Sun. →

1:30 Wedding
of Brent Yoder
Lorie Sommers

S.S. Picnic
Late p.m.
Essenhaus -
Covered bridge

Pray for
Anita

September

SEPTEMBER

S	M	T	W	T	F	S
	1	2	3	4	5	6
7	8	9	10	11	12	13
14	15	16	17	18	19	20
21	22	23	24	25	26	27
28	29	30				

OCTOBER

S	M	T	W	T	F	S
			1	2	3	4
5	6	7	8	9	10	11
12	13	14	15	16	17	18
19	20	21	22	23	24	25
26	27	28	29	30	31	

Friendship... serves a great host of different purposes all at the same time. In whatever direction you turn, it still remains yours. No barrier can shut it out. It can never be untimely; it can never be in the way. We need friendship all the time, just as much as we need the proverbial prime necessities of life, fire and water.

CICERO

21 Sunday

✓ 1:30
Communications
Fern manst
✓ Vern left @
Fammi 1:30
✓ Usher - E

24 Wednesday

✓ 9:00 Vern - hosp.
porta-cath
removed
Bone marrow
Asperation
* I drive him home
Dr. Schmucker
Call Harold B.
re: Printer
Call printer
deadline
To Jackies -
re: Carol
Ebersole's
project

25 Thursday

✓ type Auc.
✓ schedule Becky
Stenciling
Wash Windows
Clean House
Set Hosta-Mom
7:00 Carol
Ebersole

1997

22 Monday

✓ Laundry

✓ To Busk Bro. all day

✓ Work on proposal for Carol E.

23 Tuesday

✓ Finish Laundry

✓ 10:00 a.m. Mom's – 2:00 Perm

✓ lunch out @ Bob Evans

~~6:30 Meet Esther H.~~

Vern home

First training mtg.

✓ 7:00 Communications "Stewardship of Life" Comm.

Call Brenda Hostetler – Relief Sale Help

26 Friday

✓ 9–12 Bake Brownies Relief Sale

~~Call Tammy~~? ~~re: chair~~?

✓ To Nappanee – Printing

✓ To Busk Bros. w/ Carol

Relief Sale

27 Saturday

Relief Sale

Mom's Hosta

Hosta 49.00
Brass 30
79
30% – 24
$55 –

Ac 33 –
P. 22 –

plus saxifrage + brass $35 –
$9.00
30% 14.70
34.30
$35.00

Ac. 26 –
P. 9 –

September/October

SEPTEMBER

S	M	T	W	T	F	S
	1	2	3	4	5	6
7	8	9	10	11	12	13
14	15	16	17	18	19	20
21	22	23	24	25	26	27
28	29	30				

OCTOBER

S	M	T	W	T	F	S
			1	2	3	4
5	6	7	8	9	10	11
12	13	14	15	16	17	18
19	20	21	22	23	24	25
26	27	28	29	30	31	

Kindness
is a language
which the
deaf man can hear
and the
blind man read.

MARK
TWAIN

28 Sunday

✓ Usher

✓ Eugene & Gladys Springer here

✓ 4:30 – To Squeaky's w/ Al's – Merills

Call Pat Yoder – re: ~~Harvest~~ Sunday Promotion

OCTOBER

1 Wednesday

✓ Call Carol

✓ 1:00 Amy Looker Accessorizing $18.00 hr.

✓ 5:30 – Meet Carol

✓ 7:00 Members Mtg.

OCTOBER

2 Thursday

ROSH HASHANA

✓ 7:30 – Meet Pat Yoder –

✓ To Fairview ?

✓ Leta's Order

✓ Call Timmie – Deco.

1997

29 Monday

✓ 9:00 Dr. Beachy
Consult.
& filling 35.00

✓ BUSK BROS. –
12:30
Find fabrics – for Carol

8:00 Communications
Stewardship For Life
"Progress Report"

30 Tuesday

Bill Carol –

OCTOBER

3 Friday

✓ Display Glassware

✓ Deliver Leta's Plants

OCTOBER

4 Saturday

✓ Auction A.A.

Glynda Turley

October

SUN	MON	TUE	WED	THU	FRI	SAT
			1	2 Rosh Hashana	3	4
5	6	7	8	9	10	11 Yom Kippur
12	13 Columbus Day/ Thanksgiving Day (Canada)	14	15	16 National Boss Day	17	18
19	20	21	22	23	24	25
26	27	28	29	30	31	

October

OCTOBER

S	M	T	W	T	F	S
			1	2	3	4
5	6	7	8	9	10	11
12	13	14	15	16	17	18
19	20	21	22	23	24	25
26	27	28	29	30	31	

NOVEMBER

S	M	T	W	T	F	S
						1
2	3	4	5	6	7	8
9	10	11	12	13	14	15
16	17	18	19	20	21	22
23	24	25	26	27	28	29
30						

Don't judge
a book by its cover;
Or people
at first glance,
You must read
the pages of a book,
Give people a
second chance.

PHYLLIS ELLISON

5 Sunday

not ushering
October

Feet Washing
Service

8 Wednesday

Deadline – Booklet
Becky B.
stencilling

6 p.m.
Rachael & Al
Out to dinner

Type Sale Bill
Start Plants - Amy

9 Thursday

Vern to Fairview
Finish Amy's Plants
Lighting Gallery
Call Tammie – Busk Bros.
Church mail
Amy Looker
6:30
Access.
Entertainment
Center

1997

6 Monday

✓ Walk
✓ Laundry
✓ Make Poster on Computer
✓ Call Busk Bros.
✓ Work on Posters
✓ 3 P.M. - Pat Yoder picking me up - STAPLES

Call Kent B. - re: Key house

7 Tuesday

✓ Becky B. Stencilling

~~6:00 Perm~~

Plan Carol's Accessory Proposals

Take picture of Dee Birkeys

Make up photo album - Design Business

✓ Shirley - Breakfast

10 Friday

✓ Busk Bros

~~9:30 - Amy Looker Accessorizing Family Room -~~

~~(1.) oval pc. brass - mixed foliage~~

~~(2.) urn - Fireplace~~

~~(3.) lg. w/ fern (upstairs)~~

✓ 3:30 Carol E.

11 Saturday

YOM KIPPUR

October

OCTOBER

S	M	T	W	T	F	S
			1	2	3	4
5	6	7	8	9	10	11
12	13	14	15	16	17	18
19	20	21	22	23	24	25
26	27	28	29	30	31	

NOVEMBER

S	M	T	W	T	F	S
						1
2	3	4	5	6	7	8
9	10	11	12	13	14	15
16	17	18	19	20	21	22
23	24	25	26	27	28	29
30						

A true friend
warms you by her
presence,
Trusts you with
her secrets,
Remembers you
in her prayers.

ANONYMOUS

12 Sunday

15 Wednesday

Dr Traynor 10:40

Chicago

2 Ferns to Kelly in Brass

Palm to Julie

2 ivys to Kelly

16 Thursday

NATIONAL BOSS DAY

5p.m. Lindsay Volleyball

Home from Chicago

1997

13 Monday

COLUMBUS DAY / THANKSGIVING DAY (CANADA)

✓ Order (on computer) Carals furniture
✓ Church Progress Report
✓ Carol – 4 hrs.

Advance Challenge Stewardship of Life Leadership & spouses mtg. ? 7:00

14 Tuesday

1:30 Jeff Stillson

7:00 College Green Clubhouse
~~Lindsey Volleyball 5p.m. @home~~

17 Friday

✓ Contact Merrill
✓ Call Carol

~~Home from Chicago~~

18 Saturday

✓ Clean
✓ Flu shot
✓ Fix Dinner
✓ Groceries
✓ 10:00 - Meet Pat Yoder - Display case

5:00 Jim Kesher here Dinner

Upcoming Jobs

Susan's mother's kitchen
Amy - Saffitt

Quilt ~~Betty B -~~

Jackie's Windows

Plants Diane Roth?

Janette in January

Stencil Books Shirley

Jan Dressler Sten-Art
Gail Grisi
Dee - Signs 2
Designer Stencils
Royal Design Studio
Andreae Designs

October

OCTOBER

S	M	T	W	T	F	S
			1	2	3	4
5	6	7	8	9	10	11
12	13	14	15	16	17	18
19	20	21	22	23	24	25
26	27	28	29	30	31	

NOVEMBER

S	M	T	W	T	F	S
						1
2	3	4	5	6	7	8
9	10	11	12	13	14	15
16	17	18	19	20	21	22
23	24	25	26	27	28	29
30						

A good friend
is like a
wonderful book....

The inside
is even better
than the cover!

ANONYMOUS

19 Sunday

Dessert -
Shirleys
Birthday
w/merrills

22 Wednesday

✓ 10:00 Deb - Mary
Kay

Printer
✓ 1:00 Middlebury
Church Booklet

✓ 4:00 Judy Boyton
foyer ledge
Silk plants
806 Bainbridge

$20.00 hr.

23 Thursday

Chad's Birthday
✓ Order Beans
~~[illegible]~~ ?
✓ Stencil
brick pillars
✓ Order Alameda
Turkey
✓
Out to Dinner
w/Chad + Tracy
~~7:00 Worship~~
~~Comm. Mtg.~~

1997

20 Monday

~~8:00 Shirley's Birthday~~

Vote - Clubhouse

✓ Laundry

✓ Vern - Plants Out

✓ Appraisal - K

21 Tuesday

✓ Jackie

Work on lighting Accessories

meet Carol Eberanle

~~6:00~~ 7:30 ~~Dinner~~ Dessert

Doug & Janette

CAROL E.
H - 533-0724
Ofc. 535-2683

24 Friday

Stencil on Wrought Iron Fence - Frt. Room

Babysit Alexa overnite

25 Saturday

October

OCTOBER						
S	M	T	W	T	F	S
			1	2	3	4
5	6	7	8	9	10	11
12	13	14	15	16	17	18
19	20	21	22	23	24	25
26	27	28	29	30	31	

NOVEMBER						
S	M	T	W	T	F	S
						1
2	3	4	5	6	7	8
9	10	11	12	13	14	15
16	17	18	19	20	21	22
23	24	25	26	27	28	29
30						

God Almighty esteemed the life of a man in the garden the happiest He could give him, or else He would not have placed Adam in that of Eden.

SIR WILLIAM TEMPLE

Alpena News
1-800-448-0254

517-354-3111
Ext. 307
Marti

26 Sunday

3:00 Church
Flower Comm.
Wh. pillar Candles
Burgundy Sheet
Sm. Wh. Cloth

~~[illegible]~~

29 Wednesday

8:00 Prayer

To Bush
Pick up Samples

~~7:00 Judy Barton~~
~~Jane Good~~
~~3:30 Church~~
~~Re: Framework~~

unpack
inventory

30 Thursday

8:00 Prayer

1:00 Lite Gallery
1:30 Carols
Chandelier

unpack
brass

Family TV 1-800-FAMILY TV

1997

27 Monday

8:00 Prayer
To Lighting Gallery
1:00 Meet
@ Middlebury
Ervin's YC.

Mtg. w/
Jerry Landirino
1:00-4:15

6:30 - Carol (appt.)
faux - Chandelier
mirror
Total 3hrs.

28 Tuesday

8:00 Prayer
Finish Folding
E-mail 1½ hrs.
Order Catalogs
To Busk Bros.
To ~~Call~~ Gallery
Call Carol

To Liz's - Nappanee

Order Curio.
Work on Accessories
4hrs.? Jackie phone
worked on lamps } 1hr.

~~Pay Pat~~
~~25.00~~
~~Chicago~~
~~Dec. 3rd~~

~~Call Sheila~~
~~Schmucker~~

Chandelier
$450.-
my cost 360.-
90.-

8:00 Prayer
31 Friday

9:30 Jackie
Color + Cut
Bank -
Faux Boards
To Carol
P.M.
Church Booklets
Coming

Annabelle's
Plant 89.00
Hosta 17 - 89
20 37
37 52-

NOVEMBER

Key - Merrill
Paint

1 Saturday

8:00 Prayer
To Elkhart - pick up floor plans
Pie (apple
for church

9:00 Church
Usher

2-3
Carol
unlock - Merrill - lock up P.M.
get paints + primer
arrange Verlin - etc. - Mon eves
Arrange disposal of cupboards

Harvest
Meal -
Sunday
Stewardship
of Life

Judy
Boyton
533-1808

November

SUN	MON	TUE	WED	THU	FRI	SAT
						1
2	3	4	5	6	7	8
9	10	11 Veterans Day / Remembrance Day (Canada)	12	13	14	15
16	17	18	19	20	21	22
23 / 30	24	25	26	27 Thanksgiving	28	29

November

NOVEMBER

S	M	T	W	T	F	S
						1
2	3	4	5	6	7	8
9	10	11	12	13	14	15
16	17	18	19	20	21	22
23	24	25	26	27	28	29
30						

DECEMBER

S	M	T	W	T	F	S
	1	2	3	4	5	6
7	8	9	10	11	12	13
14	15	16	17	18	19	20
21	22	23	24	25	26	27
28	29	30	31			

I am once more seated under my own vine and fig tree...and hope to spend the remainder of my days...in peaceful retirement; making political pursuits yield to the more rational amusement of cultivating the earth.

GEORGE WASHINGTON

2 Sunday

"Building for Eternity" Congregational Challenge
Harvest
Dinner
no S.S.

9:00 - Usher

9:30–11:30
NO S.S.
Noon Meal

5 Wednesday

faux -
Carols
Picked up
Chandelier
repaired nail pop & filled nail holes
Finished painting wall & trim 3hrs
~~1 p.m. Church~~
~~Jane Good~~
~~Framework~~

~~helped~~ unpacking, assembly of Chandelier
assistance w/hanging Chandelier

Placement of receptacles
" Chandelier

6 Thursday

2hrs. Mirror - Clean & highlight gold
To Carol's
1 hr. hang mirror
bring Wreath home
~~Accent~~
Get art ideas together
Pick up floor lamp

Total - 4 hrs.

1997

3 Monday

✓ Laundry
~~Go to Accents~~ ~~20x20 pic.~~
~~Faux-paint for Carol — (Family Room)~~

Merrill picking up Key 4:00 - 4:30

4 Tuesday

~~9:30 Color~~

✓ Faux — Carol's

~~Pick up floor lamp @ Concord - Pennys~~
~~Take card + lamp w/me~~

Met w/electrician to assess Im. job

7 Friday

✓ Alexa coming
✓ Send Susie info.

Call:
Annabelle - Plant
Aunt Eddie
Barbara King
✓ Janette's Wreath 2 hrs.
Merrill - get Key

8 Saturday

To Mall - Mishawaka
Buy items for Harvest Sunday

~~Annabelle's Plant~~

Judy Boynton

Silk - dried arrangement

Kelly's Plants

~~Ideas to Becky Bontrager Quilt design~~

Put my ficus in brass?

Paint Chair Cream?

Doily on China Cab.

~~Plant behind my Chair?~~

November

A true friend loves at all times.

PROVERBS 17:17

Deb
10-16
Mary Kay
Open House
9-9 p.m.

NOVEMBER

S	M	T	W	T	F	S
						1
2	3	4	5	6	7	8
9	10	11	12	13	14	15
16	17	18	19	20	21	22
23	24	25	26	27	28	29
30						

DECEMBER

S	M	T	W	T	F	S
	1	2	3	4	5	6
7	8	9	10	11	12	13
14	15	16	17	18	19	20
21	22	23	24	25	26	27
28	29	30	31			

9 Sunday

Harvest Sunday - dist. food boxes

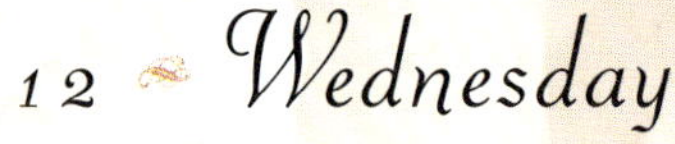

12 Wednesday

~~Fasting + Prayer room - 9 p.m. anytime in Sanctuary~~

Stencilling

✓ 4:00 Church
Jane Good
Homework

13 Thursday

✓ Everylastings w/ Shirl
Take Hosta to Annabelle
✓ Work on banner
✓ Stencil front room
✓ Baked cookies
✓ Made salad ✓

6:30 Fish Fry
Clinton Frame
Fellowship Hall
Take salad

10 Monday

✓ Laundry

✓ 4hrs. ironing

✓

Stencilling front room

Carol called re: pictures

11 Tuesday

VETERANS DAY/
REMEMBRANCE DAY (CAN)

✓ 8:30 – Dr. Beachy
Removal of Bridge

@ Carol's ofc.
Picked up Books
Took Print Door back –

Came down w/ sore throat

Paint spots underside corner

Susan's Mother's Kitchen

Picture of Dee Berkeys Bedroom

8" Clay pots
sm. ones

14 Friday

✓ Vern leaves for Fairview

✓ Stencilling

✓ To Concord Mall
✓ Rug-Kit
✓ Olivia's Xmas
✓ Bridgette's "

Sent prints to Jackie
Call to Jackie this week – 3
re: Carol's

15 Saturday

~~Wrap Wedding Gift~~

Not feeling well
Slept all day

3:00 Wedding
Clinton Frame
Eric Stutesman
Chris Ralston
Rec. Community Center
Fairgrounds

~~Do Church decor.~~
~~tomorrow evening~~

November

A true friend is one who knows all about you and loves you just as you are.
ANONYMOUS

Wagoners Nappanee Open House 14-22 9–8:30 p.m.

NOVEMBER

S	M	T	W	T	F	S
						1
2	3	4	5	6	7	8
9	10	11	12	13	14	15
16	17	18	19	20	21	22
23	24	25	26	27	28	29
30						

DECEMBER

S	M	T	W	T	F	S
	1	2	3	4	5	6
7	8	9	10	11	12	13
14	15	16	17	18	19	20
21	22	23	24	25	26	27
28	29	30	31			

16 Sunday

Commitment Sunday

Work on banner

1 hr. – 1½ hrs. ? Working @ ideas for Artwork arrangement getting order ready

19 Wednesday

Church banner

Jackie Carol - phone Frame & mat decision

20 Thursday

Stenciling Fotikon.

Bids on furn.

12:00 Meet Aunt Eddie @ Pie Pantry

Jackie Order Glynda Curley Pictures Carol ~

Lamp Pic. to Carol

1997

17 Monday

✓ Order brass - Sara ~

✓ Call Glynnda Turley Re: books, etc.

✓ Stenciling front room

✓ banner

18 Tuesday

* Accessories
Phone: Carol
Jackie
Picture decisions
sizing - vertically & horizontally
Take book to Carol

Paint Chair Cream

Ivy on China Cabinet

Carol E. -
H - 533-0724
Ofc. 535-2683

21 Friday

✓ Pick up Urn @ Aunt Eddies

✓ To Mall Xmas Shopping

Fix Gant Outfit

22 Saturday

Plant to Annabelle's

✓ 10:45 Olan Mills
Concord Mall
by Elder Beerman
4 - 8x10's 8 - Wallets for $17.80
Grandparents entitled to 5 sittings throughout year

✓ Put Thanksgiving arrangement in Church

Another Lamp
Picture to Carol

Measure Carol's mirror

touch up paint

measure left window & balance w/picture

Ornaments?

November

NOVEMBER

S	M	T	W	T	F	S
						1
2	3	4	5	6	7	8
9	10	11	12	13	14	15
16	17	18	19	20	21	22
23	24	25	26	27	28	29
30						

DECEMBER

S	M	T	W	T	F	S
	1	2	3	4	5	6
7	8	9	10	11	12	13
14	15	16	17	18	19	20
21	22	23	24	25	26	27
28	29	30	31			

We cannot tell the precise moment when friendship is formed. As in filling a vessel drop by drop, there is at last a drop which makes it run over; so in a series of kindnesses there is at last one which makes the heart run over.

JAMES BOSWELL

23 Sunday

Usher - 9:00 a.m.

Poinsettia List

Victory Sunday

First Fruits Sunday

26 Wednesday

~~Alexa here~~

In Chicago: Grandparents' Day

Shopping Xmas w/ Lindsey

~~Mix up Rolls~~

Bake Pies - one.

27 Thursday

THANKSGIVING

~~make pumpkin pie~~

Roll out Rolls

at

Kelly & Roberts

1997

24 Monday

Aleka here

Laundry
Ironing
Order Carol's Lamp Mantle
Sara's Order (2hrs.)

*Finish (2hrs.) Banner

25 Tuesday

Valeta here

~~Make Pie Crusts~~ (2)

11:30 - Cut + Wax

~~Mix up Rolls~~

4:00 Framework mtg. - have logo finished

To Chicago

Breakfast - Tom + Carolyn Dreinick

28 Friday

Home from Chicago
~~Shopping~~

Home —

29 Saturday

(Usher - Sun.)
Hang Banner
1:15 OLAN Mills
~~Sunday Dinner for Tom + Carolyn Dreinick~~

Renel's here

November/Decembe

NOVEMBER

S	M	T	W	T	F	S
						1
2	3	4	5	6	7	8
9	10	11	12	13	14	15
16	17	18	19	20	21	22
23	24	25	26	27	28	29
30						

DECEMBER

S	M	T	W	T	F	S
	1	2	3	4	5	6
7	8	9	10	11	12	13
14	15	16	17	18	19	20
21	22	23	24	25	26	27
28	29	30	31			

Let us be grateful to people who make us happy; they are the charming gardeners who make our souls blossom.

MARCEL PROUST

30 Sunday

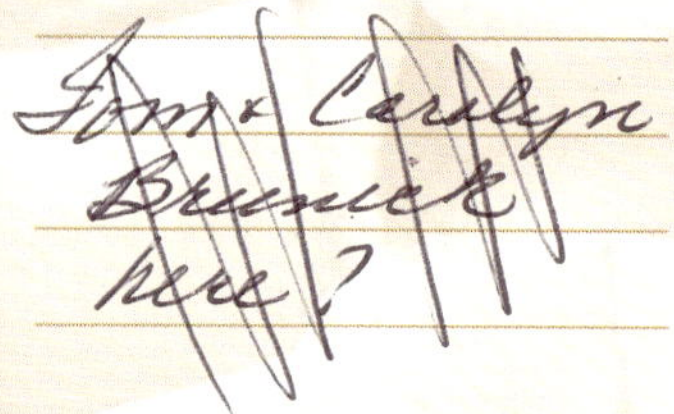

✓ Put Xmas tree up

DECEMBER

3 Wednesday

✓ To Chicago Xmas Shopping
? 7a.m. — 10 p.M
Pat Yoder
Fran Landis
~~Phyllis Mast~~
me
Jennie K.

DECEMBER

4 Thursday

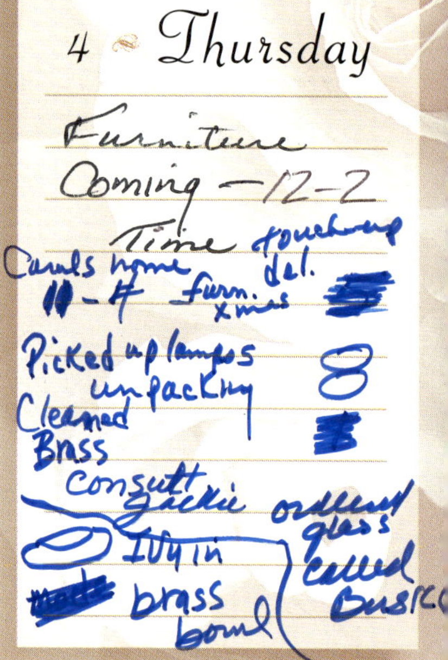

1997

DECEMBER

1 Monday

✓ 7:30
8:00 Dr. Beachy
Bridgework

Finish Xmas
Deco.

Decorate Church?
5:30 P.M.

Pick up fabric
Bask Bros.

DECEMBER

2 Tuesday

Aredia
8:00 @
registration
desk

6:00 Dinner
~~Ed~~ Doug &
Janette

DECEMBER

5 Friday

To Carols - 10 - 12:30
Packing + 2 1/2
return Lamps 45
+ mail
Pick up Glass
~~+ deliver~~ –
Ord toy chest
for Carol
Ord. new lamps

DECEMBER

6 Saturday

~~Remember Usher~~
~~Mtg. Sun. a.m.~~

1:00 - Carols
Take
glass
1 hr.

Glynda Turley ©1989

December

SUN	MON	TUE	WED	THU	FRI	SAT
	1	2	3	4	5	6
7	8	9	10	11	12	13
14	15	16	17	18	19	20
21	22	23	24 Christmas Eve / Hanukkah	25 Christmas Day	26 Boxing Day (Canada)	27
28	29	30	31			

December

DECEMBER

S	M	T	W	T	F	S
	1	2	3	4	5	6
7	8	9	10	11	12	13
14	15	16	17	18	19	20
21	22	23	24	25	26	27
28	29	30	31			

JANUARY

S	M	T	W	T	F	S
				1	2	3
4	5	6	7	8	9	10
11	12	13	14	15	16	17
18	19	20	21	22	23	24
25	26	27	28	29	30	31

I'd like to be the sort
of friend that you
have been to me,

I'd like to be the
help that you've been
always glad to be,

I'd like to mean as
much to you each
minute of the day

As you have meant,
old friend of mine, to
me along the way.

EDGAR A. GUEST

7 Sunday

8:15 -
Usher Mtg.
@ church

10 Wednesday

Jackie
Coming
Accessories

Jackie 9-3 5 hrs.
me - 4 hrs.

11 Thursday

~~V.S. Elsie Meyers~~
~~537-4676~~
~~119 Professional~~
~~Pickup at 9:10~~

Pickup Glass end tab.
Plan - Hang quilt ensemble
Place plants
Christmas Tree Decor.
Lunch
w/ Aunt Eddie
Lee & Ruby
Shantz

1997

8 Monday

Laundry
To DR.- Bronchitis
Order glass -
Carol's end tables
28" dia.

Call Kline's - Throw

Set Several Plants

9 Tuesday

8:00 a.m. Perm?
Perm, if needed
8:30 Color

Slept a lot

Groom plants
Set plants
4:00 - Tracy's
To Busk Bros 1 hr.
Worship Comm.
Mtg. 7 p.m.

DR. BORON
Gastroenterologist
296-3341

12 Friday

Elkhart Clinic
Nappanee St.
8:30 appt. 8:45

Cimarrutta
Cimarrutta
Doug + Janette
John + Dee
Chap. + Jennie
Kauffman
Vern + L

2:15 Elva Gascho
#4, F.T. entrance

13 Saturday

Colby - game
Grant - game

Mr. Periwinkle's
XMAS Party
w/ Al +
Rachael
Oakwood
Inn

6:15

December

There's a miracle
called friendship
That dwells
within the heart,
And you don't know
how it happens
Or when it gets
its start.
But the happiness
it brings you
Always gives a
special lift,
And you realize
that friendship
Is life's most
precious gift.

ANONYMOUS

DECEMBER

S	M	T	W	T	F	S
	1	2	3	4	5	6
7	8	9	10	11	12	13
14	15	16	17	18	19	20
21	22	23	24	25	26	27
28	29	30	31			

JANUARY

S	M	T	W	T	F	S
				1	2	3
4	5	6	7	8	9	10
11	12	13	14	15	16	17
18	19	20	21	22	23	24
25	26	27	28	29	30	31

14 Sunday

Address Xmas Cards

17 Wednesday

~~10:00 Color x Cut~~

Chicago – Check-up Vern 10:40

18 Thursday

5:00 ~~8:00~~ Dr. Beachy new Bridge

Called Service - Jill wrong fabric 2nd time!

To Elkhart - paper wt. folks money

1997

15 Monday

Laundry

Work on Xmas cards

✓ 1-3 - Meet Busk for repairs @ Carols

Buy Kent Miller gift

16 Tuesday

✓ Finish Xmas cards

✓ S.S. Class-Xmas

Call Andy Stoner FW

✓ Finish Banner

✓ Type up mock cover

Check Staples yellow paper 1000 - Buy

✓ 4:00 Framework

Andy Stoner Ft. Wayne

Call UMA re: Candlesholder w/glass globes

19 Friday

VA. ✓ 2:20 health care whol Patients

✓ Clean House

✓ Kent - A.M. will call proposal

~~1 PM - 6 PM Blood Mobile Clinton Frame 1-800 GIVE LIFE~~

5:00 Poinsettias in place

20 Saturday

Poinsettias

✓ Put banner up

✓ 2 doz. cookies (church)

✓ Meal - Lasagna 5 PM Bill & Karen Wunt

3/4 mi. yellow house green shutters

24

Electrolux

13

December

The person who sows seeds of kindness enjoys a perpetual harvest.

VERN McLELLAN

DECEMBER

S	M	T	W	T	F	S
	1	2	3	4	5	6
7	8	9	10	11	12	13
14	15	16	17	18	19	20
21	22	23	24	25	26	27
28	29	30	31			

JANUARY

S	M	T	W	T	F	S
				1	2	3
4	5	6	7	8	9	10
11	12	13	14	15	16	17
18	19	20	21	22	23	24
25	26	27	28	29	30	31

21 Sunday

Chad & Tracy went to Church w/us

To: JACKIES
Vern -
GER. PRAYER Church

24 Wednesday

CHRISTMAS EVE/ HANUKKAH

MAKE FOOD
- Bake Pecan Pies
- make AuGratin
- Ribbon Salad

Meet @ 5:00
Light Votives

Christmas Eve. Service
Gingerbread w/orange fluff
Ray & Fran - Chas. & Jennie, Squeaks & Vesda

25 Thursday

CHRISTMAS DAY

Set table - 16
Broccoli-Chees
ROLLS
Kids Coming

Christmas Dinner
1:00 P.M. - also
Aunt Eddie

1997

22 Monday

Laundry

Get Groceries

Make Tea Rings

23 Tuesday

✓ Took paper wt. back

✓ Cedar boughs on Chandelier?

✓ Water Poinsettias

✓ make Praline Yams

✓ Mix up rolls

✓ Crafts - Kids

CHRISTMAS DINNER

17 peo.
w/ Aunt Eddie
Kent Miller

✓ HAM - TURKEY •

✓ PRALINE YAMS •

✓ AUGRATIN POT. W

✓ RIBBON SALAD W

✓ BROCCOLI

~~ARTICHOKES~~

~~w/ [illegible]~~

ROLLS ~~dip~~ •

Relishes

Pecan Pie W

26 Friday

BOXING DAY (CANADA)

Breakfast

Sausage Egg Casserole

T - Rasp. Jam

Tea Ring

27 Saturday

December/January

Blessed are they who have the gift of making friends, for it is one of God's best gifts. It involves many things, but above all, the power of going out of one's self and appreciating whatever is noble and loving in another.

THOMAS HUGHES

DECEMBER

S	M	T	W	T	F	S
	1	2	3	4	5	6
7	8	9	10	11	12	13
14	15	16	17	18	19	20
21	22	23	24	25	26	27
28	29	30	31			

JANUARY

S	M	T	W	T	F	S
				1	2	3
4	5	6	7	8	9	10
11	12	13	14	15	16	17
18	19	20	21	22	23	24
25	26	27	28	29	30	31

28 Sunday

31 Wednesday

Marshall Antique Auction

JANUARY

1 Thursday
NEW YEAR'S DAY

Marshall Antique Auction

1997

29 Monday

9:00 To Pams + Todd – Bring Portfolio

30 Tuesday

Take Barbara King - S.B.

1-6 - Haircut 3:00 PM

* Important! 6 mo. Dentist Check-up 10:30 Tues. 1-6-98 Dr. Beachy 110 W. High Pt. 533-5926

1-2-98 9:15 Dr. Kay Karen - Pap - breast -

Jan 13 - Momm.

Couples Retreat Mar. 27-28-29

Chicago Mkt Jan '17-24?

1-6 Tues. meet Eli + Paula S. Pleasant Village

Jan 13 - Tues. 4:00 Frame work

JANUARY

2 Friday

9:15 Dr. Kay Breast, Pap

Carol M. Shirley C. Coming

JANUARY

3 Saturday

til mon.?

Addresses & Phone Numbers

Mary Kay
Deb Handrich — (219) 534-3534
608 E. Kercher Rd.

David Kay, M.D. — (219) 533-9009
101 Marilyn Ave. — (219) 534-3102 FAX
Suite 3
Goshen, IN 46526

Schrock Homes
ALL Offices — 533-1148 ALL OFFICES

First Impressions
Jackie — 534-1806

Addresses & Phone Numbers

Mary Showalter
Creative Touch Decorating 219-457-8510
Painting - Wallpapering Milford

Nancy McEllery 800-873-3644
Elkhart 46515 219-522-6007
P.O. Box 2722

Connie Welcher 825-9471
Ext. 450
Essenhaus Decorator

Stencillusions (718) 634-4415
V+ Olga Decorating
159 Beach 123 rd St.
Rockaway Park, NY
11694

Addresses & Phone Numbers

Addresses & Phone Numbers

Addresses & Phone Numbers

Addresses & Phone Numbers

Birthdays & Anniversaries

Notes

Notes

Notes

Notes